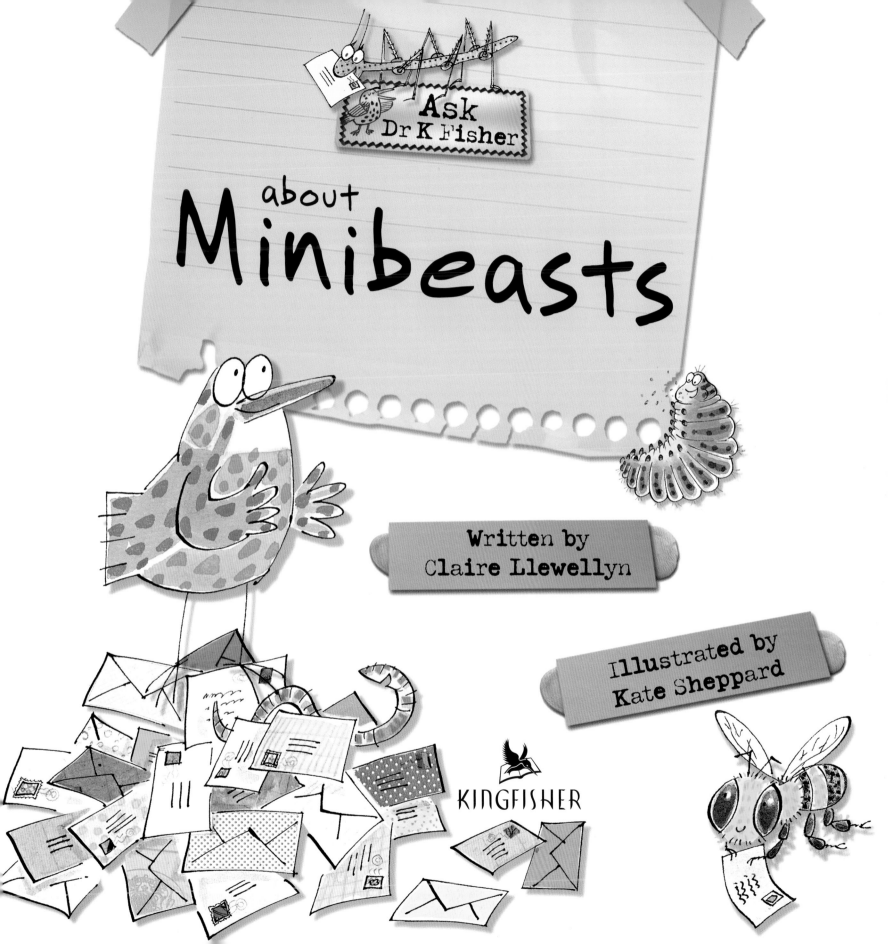

Ask Dr K Fisher

about Minibeasts

Written by
Claire Llewellyn

Illustrated by
Kate Sheppard

KINGFISHER

Claire

Kate

🦅 KINGFISHER

First published 2008 by Kingfisher
an imprint of Macmillan Children's Books
a division of Macmillan Publishers Ltd
4 Crinan Street London N1 9XW
Basingstoke and Oxford
Associated companies throughout the world
www.panmacmillan.com

Consultant: David Burnie

ISBN: 978-0-7534-1574-0

9 8 7 6 5 4 3 2 1
1RD/0908/MPA/SCHOY(MPA)/157MA/C

A CIP catalogue record for this book is available from the British Library.

Printed in China

For Samuel, with love – C.L.
For William – K.S.

Kingfisher,

Macmillan Children's Books,

4 Crinan Street,

London N1 9XW

www.panmacmillan.com

Ask Dr K Fisher about...

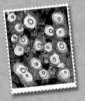

Dogs beware!

Dear Dr K Fisher,

I'm a male scorpion and I live in the desert. I've always been shy about being so small (I'm only a few centimetres from tip to tail). The other day a friend told me that, tiny or not, the sting I have in my tail could kill a dog in seven minutes. Is this true or was he just being kind? Maybe I should test it out. If so, where can I get a dog? Around here, they are hard to find.

Small but Hopeful,
in the Sahara desert

dog

scorpion

beetles

Dr K Fisher
Any problem solved!
1 Diving-in-the-Water,
Birdsville KF1 1YZ

Dear **Small but Hopeful,**

It's true, you do carry a deadly poison in the sting at the end of your tail. If you start using it to prove your strength, though, you'll soon tire yourself out and get caught by a lizard or snake. You don't need your sting to catch beetles – your strong pincers and sharp jaws do the job perfectly well. Your sting is there to save your life if you come under attack. Your body uses up a lot of energy to produce venom, so try not to waste a drop. Dogs are not your enemy: if you do see one, please leave it alone!

Best wishes,

Dr K Fisher

Here's an *unhappy earthworm*

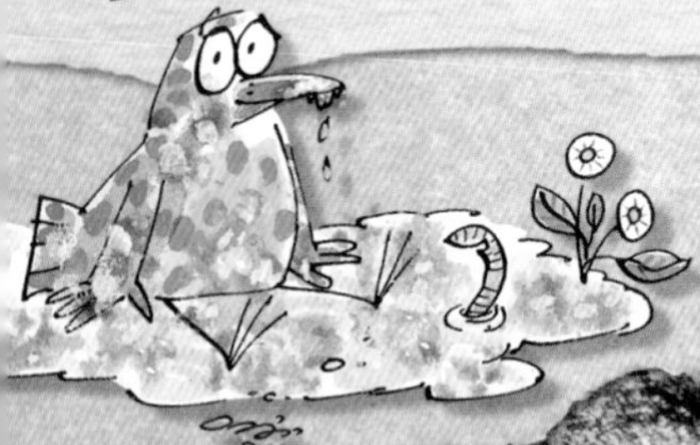

Bored with my body

Dear Dr K Fisher,

I'm an earthworm and I'm feeling depressed. Why? Well, take a look at me, if you can bear to. I'm just a tube with lots of segments. I have no eyes, no wings, no feelers and no legs. Why do I have this boring, boring body?

Feeling Down,
under the lawn

tunnel

earthworm

bird

Dr K Fisher
Any problem solved!
1 Diving-in-the-Water,
Birdsville KF1 1YZ

Dear **Feeling Down,**

You have the perfect body for life underground. Your long, smooth shape helps you burrow through the earth, while your segments contain powerful muscles that pull and push you along. They also help you hold on tight when birds try to tug you from the ground. Cheer up! You worms are important animals. As you feed on mud and rotting plants, your body breaks them down into a fine, fertile soil. And your tunnels let in plenty of oxygen and water, making the soil the perfect place for healthy plants to grow.

Yours truly,

Dr K Fisher

Turn the page for **more** on **minibeast bodies...**

Dr K Fisher's Guide to Minibeast Bodies

There are many **different** groups of minibeasts, including snails, worms, **millipedes, spiders** and insects. Each group has its own special body **plan**.

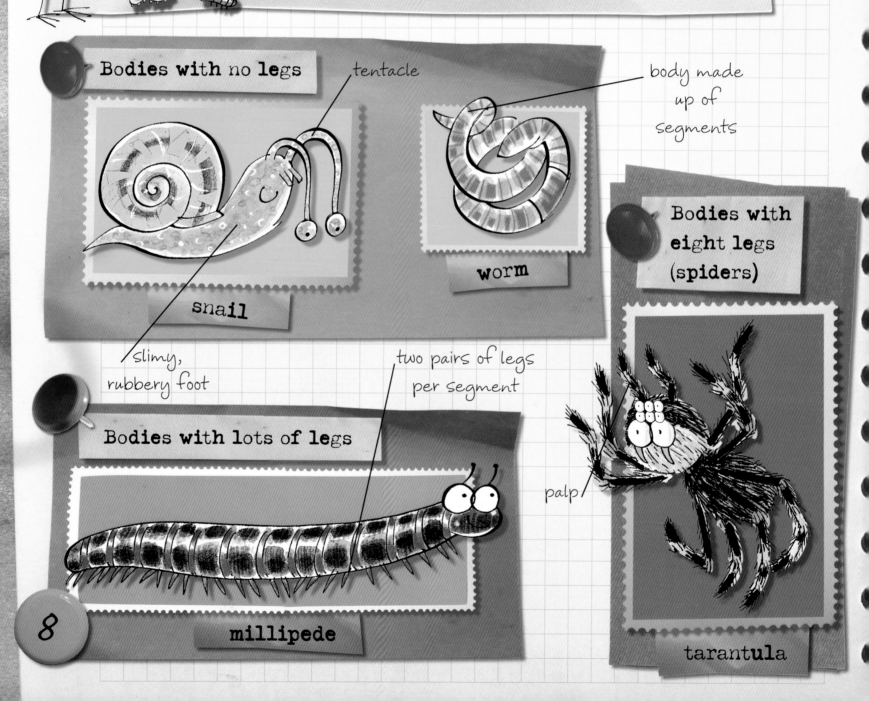

Bodies with no legs

tentacle

body made up of segments

snail

slimy, rubbery foot

worm

Bodies with eight legs (spiders)

Bodies with lots of legs

two pairs of legs per segment

palp

millipede

tarantula

Bodies with six legs, and made up of the head, thorax and abdomen (insects)

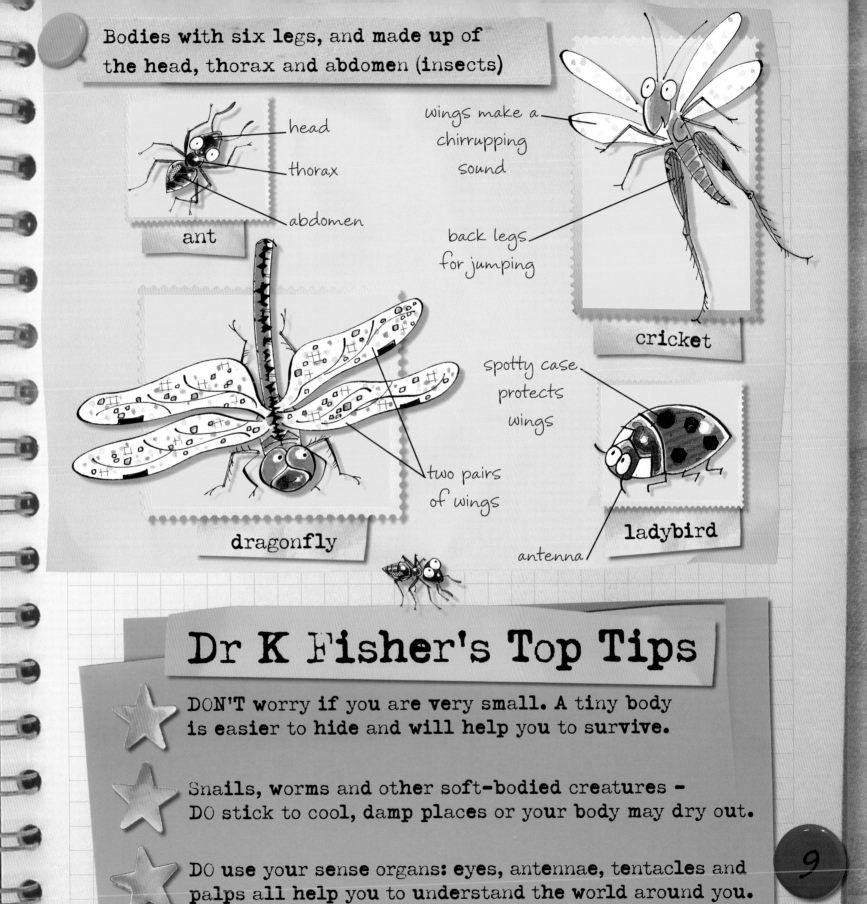

head

thorax

abdomen

ant

wings make a chirrupping sound

back legs for jumping

cricket

two pairs of wings

dragonfly

spotty case protects wings

ladybird

antenna

Dr K Fisher's Top Tips

★ **DON'T** worry if you are **very** small. A tiny body is easier to **hide** and **will help** you to **survive**.

★ Snails, worms and other soft-bodied creatures – **DO** stick to cool, damp places or your body may dry out.

★ **DO** **use** your **sense** organs: eyes, antennae, tentacles and palps all **help** you to **understand** the **world** around you.

Turn off the light!

Dear Dr K Fisher,

I'm a female glow-worm and I have an embarrassing problem. I just can't stop blushing. Whenever I'm out on warm summer nights, my abdomen flashes with a bright yellow glow. I can't seem to control it! I think the moths and crickets are laughing at me. Please, please, please help me cure this horrible habit.

Bothered by Blushes,
at twilight

moth

cricket

female
glow-worm

10

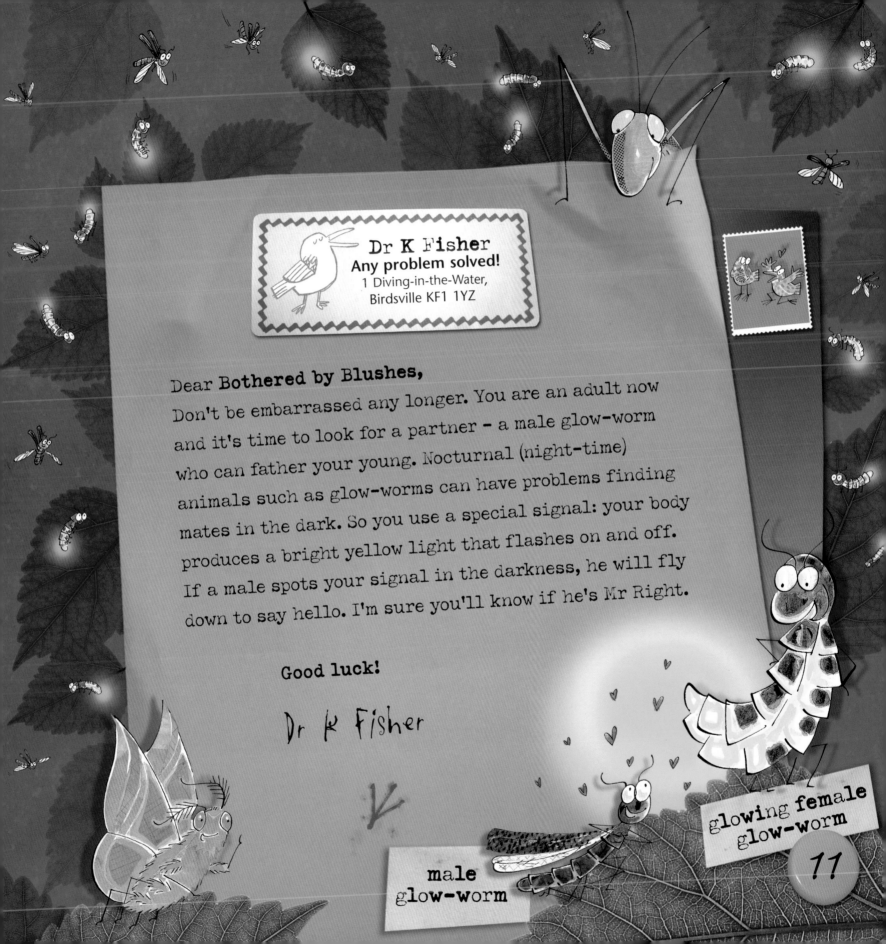

Dr K Fisher
Any problem solved!
1 Diving-in-the-Water,
Birdsville KF1 1YZ

Dear **Bothered by Blushes,**

Don't be embarrassed any longer. You are an adult now and it's time to look for a partner – a male glow-worm who can father your young. Nocturnal (night-time) animals such as glow-worms can have problems finding mates in the dark. So you use a special signal: your body produces a bright yellow light that flashes on and off. If a male spots your signal in the darkness, he will fly down to say hello. I'm sure you'll know if he's Mr Right.

Good luck!

Dr K Fisher

male
glow-worm

glowing female
glow-worm

11

A need for speed!

Dear Dr K Fisher,
I'm a millipede, and I'm feeling humiliated. My cousin's a cocky centipede and last week I challenged him to a race. (I've got more legs than him so I thought I'd win.) But he overtook me straightaway! Now he wants a re-match and I'm bound to lose. Help!
Feel-like-a-loser,
in the leaves

millipede

THE WOODLAND
23RD AUG
POST

Dr K Fisher,

1 Diving-in-the-Water,

Birdsville,

KF1 1YZ

Finish Line

centipede

Dr K Fisher
Any problem solved!
1 Diving-in-the-Water,
Birdsville KF1 1YZ

Dear **Feel-like-a-loser**,

Your centipede cousin needs his speed. He's a carnivore and has to catch other minibeasts to eat. You millipedes are herbivores, munching mainly on dead leaves that can't run away. Yes, you have more legs than your cousin. Millipedes have four legs on each segment of your body, while centipedes have only two on each segment. But they wriggle fast over the ground while you crawl slowly. Avoid another race – just tell him you're busy. Try not to annoy him, though, as he has sharp jaws and poisonous fangs. If he gets nasty, curl up until he goes away.

Best wishes,

Dr K Fisher

millipede enjoying an easy meal

13

Battle of the bulge

Dear Dr K Fisher,

I'm a caterpillar and I'm worried about myself. My body has grown alarmingly and my skin's so tight I feel it's going to burst. Could my eating habits be to blame? I feed all day on juicy green leaves — they are surprisingly delicious — and I just can't stop. Do you think this could be the problem?

Always Hungry,

in the Leaves

caterpillar about to burst

butterfly

Dear **Always Hungry,**

What you describe is perfectly normal. Like many minibeasts, you have a tough, outer skin called the exoskeleton, which protects your body. As you feed and grow, this skin regularly splits, and underneath there is a new skin in a larger size. The fifth time this happens, you change into a pupa, a new, exciting stage in your life, when your body develops into its adult form. After two weeks, you will crawl out as a butterfly. You'll feed from flowers instead of leaves, and you'll have a wonderful set of wings.

Good luck!

Dr K Fisher

Almost there!

egg

pupa

Turn the page for **more** on **insect wings...**

15

caterpillar

Dr K Fisher's Guide to Insect Wings

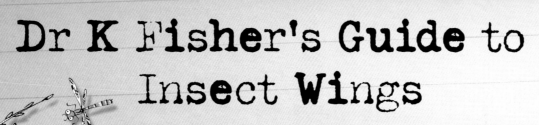

Most adult insects have wings and can fly. Flying helps them to hunt, find a mate and escape from danger. The different types of wings provide each of the insects on this page with the perfect flying kit.

A **butterfly** has two pairs of wings. They shimmer beautifully in the light – perfect for attracting a mate!

Wasps have two pairs of small, delicate wings. They are ideal for flying fast.

wasp

morpho butterfly

Dragonflies are expert fliers with two pairs of strong wings. They can hover, shoot up or down, or even fly backwards.

This beetle has fragile flying wings. When it's on the ground, it tucks them under its hard wing cases.

Flies have just one pair of wings. They beat so fast that they buzz.

Atlas beetle

fly

dragonfly

Dr K Fisher's Top Tips

★ DO take care of your wings. They are so important to you, but are fragile and easily damaged.

★ DO find a good place to take off into the air. The top of a flower stalk makes a great launch site.

★ DON'T forget to feed frequently. It takes a lot of energy to fly.

17

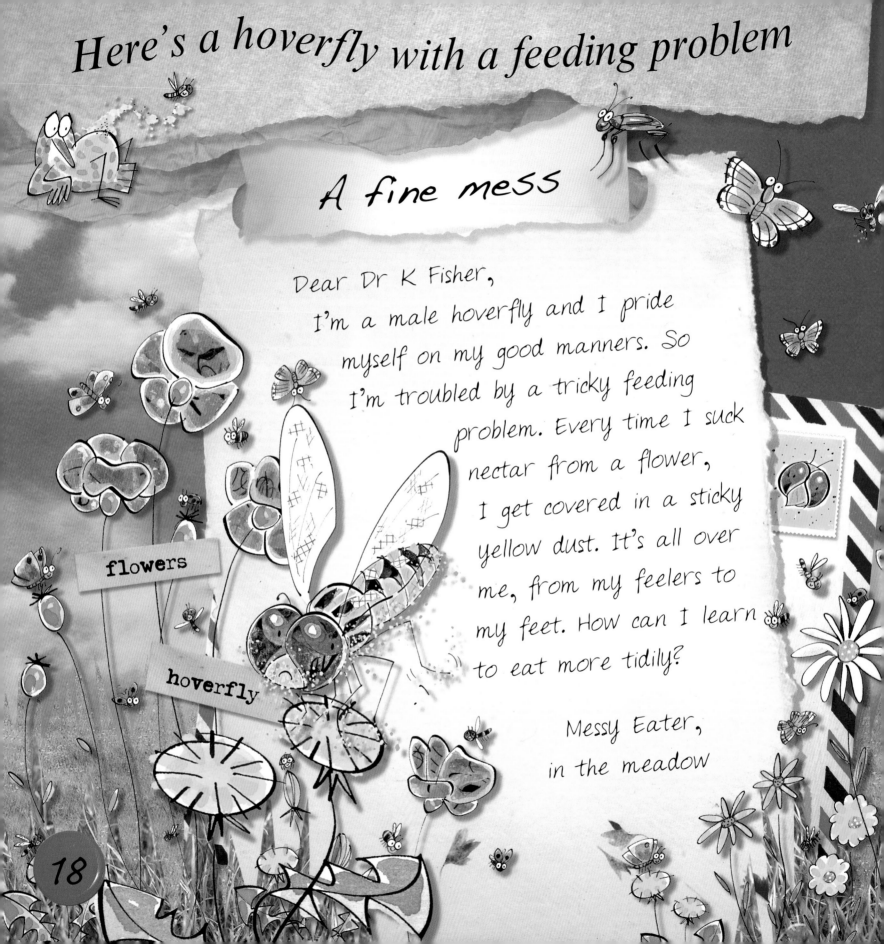

A fine mess

Dear Dr K Fisher,

I'm a male hoverfly and I pride myself on my good manners. So I'm troubled by a tricky feeding problem. Every time I suck nectar from a flower, I get covered in a sticky yellow dust. It's all over me, from my feelers to my feet. How can I learn to eat more tidily?

Messy Eater,
in the meadow

flowers

hoverfly

Dr K Fisher
Any problem solved!
1 Diving-in-the-Water,
Birdsville KF1 1YZ

Dear **Messy Eater,**

Don't worry: it's impossible for you to drink nectar without picking up pollen, too. Pollen (that's the name for the sticky yellow dust) helps plants to make seeds, but first it must be moved from flower to flower. Plants can't move the pollen themselves, so most get insects to do it for them. As you feed, you pick up the pollen, which rubs off when you visit the next flower. You are doing an important job: every time you pollinate a flower, you are helping new seeds to grow.

Best wishes,

Dr K Fisher

helpful hoverfly

other pollinating insects at work

19

Here's a worried stick insect

Oh brother!

Dear Dr K Fisher,

I'm a male stick insect and I'm concerned about my brother. A week ago, we were sitting side by side, but when I turned round he'd disappeared, and I haven't seen him since. It's tricky finding him on this bush. Whenever I think I've spotted him, 'he' turns out to be a twig. There are geckos and birds round here, and I'm worried they'll catch the little chap. What do you think I should do?

Fretting about Family,
in the forest

stick insect

Dr K Fisher
Any problem solved!
1 Diving-in-the-Water,
Birdsville KF1 1YZ

Dear **Fretting about Family,**

Try not to worry about your brother. Stick insects have long, brown, slender bodies, which blend in perfectly against branches and twigs and are almost impossible to spot. This camouflage is such a brilliant defence that predators are unlikely to catch your brother. Unfortunately, this means that you, too, are unlikely to find him, unless you're very lucky, and patient, and you manage to catch him actually moving.

Yours sincerely,

Dr K Fisher

golden gecko (predator!)

Found **him!**

Turn the page for **more** on **insect disguises...**

21

Dr K Fisher's Guide to Insect Disguises

Insects are the masters of disguise. All the insects on this page have developed camouflage to blend in with their surroundings. This allows them to hide from predators or prey. They're all hard to spot!

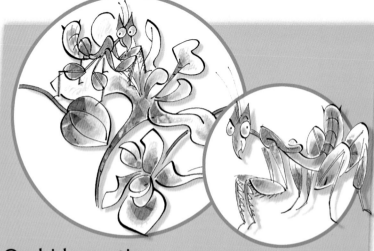

Leaf insect

Habitat: Tropical rainforests

Camouflage: Body shape and colour make it look like a leaf.

How it works: Predators do not recognize the insect as food, and leave it alone.

Bonus: If grabbed, a leaf insect can shed a leg and make a quick escape.

Spotted? I spotted him last week.

Orchid mantis

Habitat: Tropical rainforests

Camouflage: Pink body and petal-shaped legs blend in against orchid flowers.

How it works: Mantis hides on the flower, waiting to gobble up insects that feed there.

Bonus: Its clever camouflage keeps it hidden from predators, too.

Spotted? What a clever disguise!

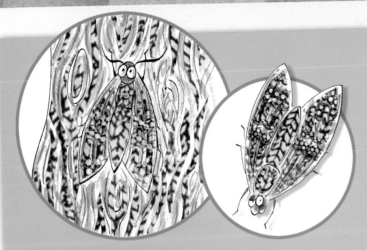

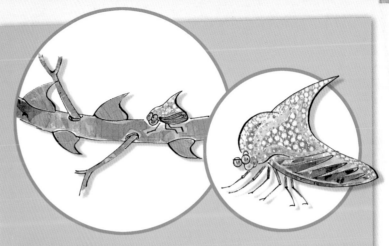

Pine hawkmoth

Habitat: Pine forests

Camouflage: Dull, blotchy wings that blend in with tree bark.

How it works: Allows it to rest on a tree in the daytime without being spotted.

Bonus: As a caterpillar, the hawkmoth has a different disguise – as a pine needle.

Spotted? ◯ I haven't seen this one yet.

Thorn bug

Habitat: The stems of young tropical trees.

Camouflage: Hard, triangular, pointed body looks like a thorn.

How it works: Predators don't see it. They mistake it for part of the plant.

Bonus: Predators dislike the thorn bug's hard, spiky body, which is painful to eat.

Spotted? ✔ Ouch – he's sharp!

Dr K Fisher's Top Tips

DON'T move a millimetre! Camouflage only works if you keep very still.

DON'T feed during the daytime when predators can see you. It's much safer to feed at night.

Remember, eggs and droppings can give you away. DON'T leave them near your hiding place.

Here's a worn-out spider

What an effort!

squirrel monkey (web destroyer!)

Dear Dr K Fisher,

I'm a female spider and I'm feeling fed up. Early every morning I make a web. Spinning silk is a tricky business and I work hard to get it right. But most days, my web ends up in tatters – animals blunder into it, or it gets spoilt by the wind and rain. I end up having to destroy it myself and start again the next day. Surely there are easier ways to catch a meal?

Wasting a Lifetime,
on the web

golden silk orb-web spider

Dr K Fisher
Any problem solved!
1 Diving-in-the-Water,
Birdsville KF1 1YZ

Dear **Wasting a Lifetime,**

A sticky web is a great way to catch flying insects, and is building one really so hard? A web like yours only takes about an hour. It's true you have to renew it most days, but at least you can eat the old one up and recycle the precious silk. There are other ways of catching a meal. Some spiders build traps and ambush their prey; others simply jump on it, but they have better eyesight than you. Spinning a web is a real talent – I would stick with it, if I were you.

Best wishes,

Dr K Fisher

25

Here's a hard-working honey bee

Give me a rest!

larva

pupa

queen bee

worker feeding larvae

Dear Dr K Fisher,

I'm a female honey bee and all
I ever do is work, work, work. We girls
never stop: we have to clean the nest,
look after the eggs, larvae and pupae,
search for nectar, make honey AND feed
the queen. Meanwhile, she and
the drones, the lazy male bees,
never do a thing. I'm fed up with
being a slave. What do
you think I should do?

Hot and Bothered,
in the nest

summer: females working outside

busy female worker bee

winter:
goodbye, guys!

Dr K Fisher
Any problem solved!
1 Diving-in-the-Water,
Birdsville KF1 1YZ

Dear **Hot and Bothered,**

Honey bees live in a colony – a huge team that pulls together to build a home, find food, fend off enemies and care for the young. You and the other female bees work hard all summer, inside the nest and out. The queen, poor thing, lays eggs all day. It's true that the drones, or male bees, have an easy life at the moment, but they will be kicked out of the nest in winter to shiver in the cold. Then the females will dine on tasty honey and enjoy a well-deserved rest.

Good luck!

Dr K Fisher

winter: females
having a rest!

Dr K Fisher's Guide to Insect Colonies

Some insects **live** in groups called colonies. In a colony, **all the insects** work as a **team** to **build** and **look after the nest. The** ants on **this page** are part of one colony. Each ant **has special** jobs to do.

Queen's quarters

A royal room! The large queen ant spends her whole life laying eggs.

Boys-only den

Male ants mate with the queen, but spend most of their time resting.

Building site

Workers hollow out the nest and build new tunnels.

Dr K Fisher's Top Tips

★ **DON'T** let your colony get too crowded. If it does, some of you should fly off in a swarm and start a new one.

★ **DO** build your nest **where predators won't easily find it – in a cave, a hollow tree or under the ground.**

★ **DO** build your nest **with the right materials: wax for bees, chewed-up wood for wasps and soil for ants.**

Nursery 1
Workers (females) take the new eggs to a safe place to hatch.

Nursery 2
Workers are busy feeding the larvae.

Nursery 3
Workers make sure the pupae are safe and warm.

Glossary

abdomen
The back part of a minibeast's body.

antenna
A feeler that picks up scents on the air, and helps minibeasts move around.

camouflage
A shape, colour or pattern that helps an animal to hide.

carnivore
A meat-eating animal.

colony
A large group of animals that live together.

disguise
A shape, colour or pattern that makes a minibeast look like something else, so it can escape danger.

drone
A male honey bee.

fertile
Good, rich soil where lots of plants can grow.

fragile
Easily ruined.

herbivore
A plant-eating animal.

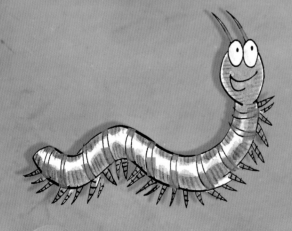

insect
A type of minibeast that has six legs.

larva
The second stage in an insect's life, after it has hatched out of an egg.